Star Craft

a "how to" guide for creating the Froebel paper star (and more!)

written, illustrated, and photographed by **Frances Martin**

Star Craft

a "how to" guide for creating the Froebel paper star (and more!)
Frances Martin

ISBN

Thank you to my husband, Shawn, and my boys, Kian and Brendan, for supporting me through all my star folding days.

"Mommy put your paper down!"

I would also like to express my sincere appreciation to all of my customers who have made requests that have pushed and expanded my creativity. I wouldn't have written this book without you.

Contents

vintage cross and christmas stars made by my great-grandmother

In the early 60's my grandmother gave my great-grandmother the directions on how to fold a Froebel star that she had found in a Woman's Day magazine. My great-grandmother made many stars for her church and her family's Christmas trees. In 1997 my mother was given a vintage box of ornaments made by my great-grandmother and so began our legacy in making the paper star.

In my early days I hand cut poster board sheets and soon after, invested in a paper cutter. I first began selling my stars in my mother's massage therapy and natural gift shop in 2002. After the birth of my first son I spent more time at home and opened my Etsy site in 2007.

Since then I have experimented with other things that can be made from the Froebel stars. Most of which I have included in this book.

The Froebel star was invented by Freidrich Frobel, who also invented kindergarten. He created mathematical paper folding exercises in an attempt to empower children to be lively and free by providing them with material to engage in self-directed activity. These activities then in turn taught the children to use his or her environment as an educational aid. (information found on wikipedia.com)

The Froebel Star has spread through cultures worldwide and also has been known as the Moravian Star, Christmas Star, Herrnhut Star, Advent Star, German Star, Ribbon Star, Danish Star, Swedish Star, and Pennsylvania Star. Folded paper stars have appear in northern Europe where they were traditionally made with white paper. These crafty works of art are not really origami, but closer to a form of basketry. They are woven and folded from four long strips of paper, dipped in melted paraffin, and sprinkled with glitter to create a three dimensional, sixteen-pointed star. The stars were originally hung outside to decorate evergreen and shrubbery during the holiday season. The intent of dipping these stars in wax was a weather proofing technique to keep the stars from rain and snow damage. Through the years they have become more than just Christmas decorations; each folded paper star is a work of art.

Chapter 1
History of the Froebel star

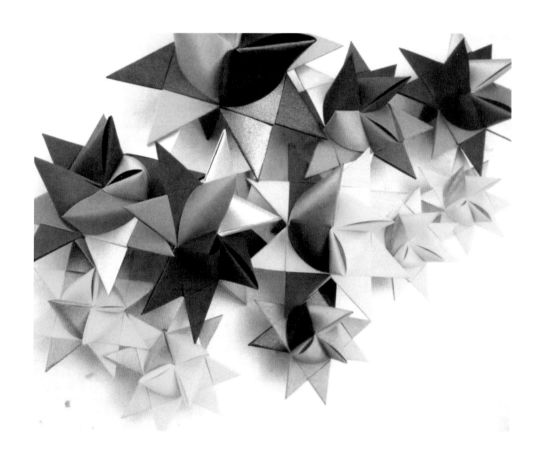

Chapter 2
How to fold the Moravian star

Step 1
Take four strips of paper and fold them in half width-wise. Trim the open edges (not the folded edge) for ease of threading the papers through themselves.

Step 5
Then thread the third strip through the center of the first strip.

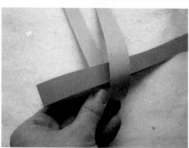

Step 2
Take one strip with the folded edge on your left. Take a second strip with the fold on the bottom and close it around the first strip.

Step 6
Pull all the strips tight against each other making a woven square.

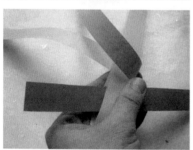

Step 3
Take a third strip with the fold on the right and close it around the second strip.

Step 7
Flip the square over.

Step 4
Take the last strip with the fold at the top and close it around the third strip.

Step 8
Fold the top upper strip down and crease.

Step 9
Fold the top left strip to the right and crease.

Step 13
Pull tight and crease, making an interlocked square weave.

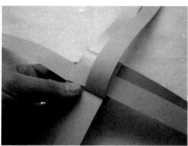

Step 10
Fold the top bottom strip up and crease.

Step 14
To create the points around the outside of the star, take an upper right strip and fold it back away from you at an angle to the right. Keep it flush with the square weave and crease.

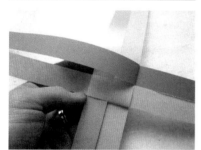

Step 11
Fold the top right strip to the left and crease.

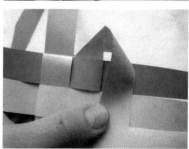

Step 15
Take that same strip and fold towards you at an angle and down, keeping it flush.

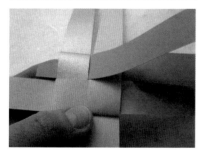

Step 12
Thread the end of that strip through the the loop that was created from folding the top upper right strip down.

Step 16
Take the strip and fold it like turning the page of a book over to the right and crease.

Step 17
Bend the point back enough to see the top right loop on the square weave.

Step 21
Rotate the star clockwise a quarter of a turn and repeat steps 14 through 19.

Step 18
Take the end of the strip and thread it through the loop.

Step 22
Rotate the star clockwise a quarter of a turn and repeat steps 14 through 19, be sure the last strip goes through the loop. It will be behind the strip coming out from the center of the square weave.

Step 19
Pull the strip through, be sure not to pull the point clear through the loop.

First side complete.

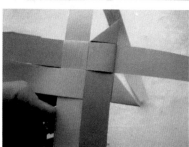

Step 20
Rotate the star clockwise a quarter of a turn and repeat steps 14 through 19.

Step 23
Flip the star over.

Step 24
Repeat steps 14 thru 19.

Eight points complete.

Step 25
Rotate the star clockwise a quarter of a turn and repeat steps 14 through 19.

Step 28
Fold all 4 strips back towards their points and crease.

Step 26
Rotate the star clockwise a quarter of a turn and repeat steps 14 through 19.

Step 29
Take one of the strips and loop it around on top of its same color.

Step 27
Repeat step 20, be sure the last strip goes through the loop. It will be behind the strip coming out from the center of the square weave.

Step 30
Keeping the SAME SIDE of the strip UP, tuck the end through the slot under the upper folded strip.

Step 31
Pull taunt.

One side complete.

Step 32
Rotate the star counter clockwise a quarter of a turn and repeat steps 29 through 31.

Step 35
Flip star over and repeat steps 28 thru 34. Both sides complete.

Step 33
Rotate the star counter clockwise a quarter of a turn and repeat steps 29 through 31.

Step 36
Trim strips flush with the points from which they are extending.

Step 34
Rotate the star counter clockwise a quarter of a turn and repeat steps 29 through 31.

Completed star.
I also have a youtube video at: http://www.youtube.com/watch?v=P-HMJiRg1kk

Chapter 3
Stringing, waxing, glittering, and ribboned stars

You can purchase paraffin wax at
your local craft store. It can be
found in the candle sections sold
in blocks of various poundage.

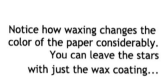
Notice how waxing changes the
color of the paper considerably.
You can leave the stars
with just the wax coating...

Heat the wax directly on the stove
over medium heat until melted.

or glitter the stars that have been
waxed before the wax dries...

You will know when the wax is hot enough because
the paper starts to sizzle and bubble with placed in
the wax. Turn the wax on low or off at this point.

or totally saturate with glitter
that is similar color as the paper.

Flip star over in the wax to get both sides coated,
then place on a brown paper bag or cardboard shirt
box to dry. Be sure to flip star over as it dries to
keep wax bubbles from globbing up on the tips that
touch the drying surface.

Spheres can be done in the same way.

To string stars take a needle and poke it through one of the corners of the star. Wiggle it around so it opens where the hole goes through.

Then pull down the top of the ribbon and tuck it behind the part where the ribbon crisscrosses. Going upward, pierce the ribbon clear through two times so that it comes out at the top.

Push filament thread through the hole, pull through, and trim to desired length. Use plyers to close crimp bead in place.

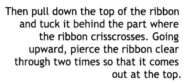

Thread both ends of an already strung star through the eye of the needle and pull through the ribbon.

Ribboned stars are made by first taking your ribbon in a loop as shown.

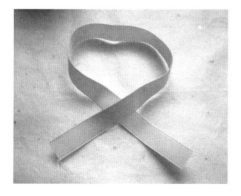

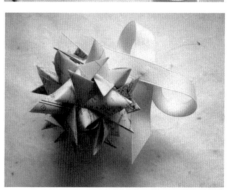

Push ribbon close to the star and use pliers to close crimp bead in place.

 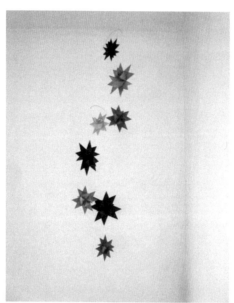 

Chapter 4
Mobiles

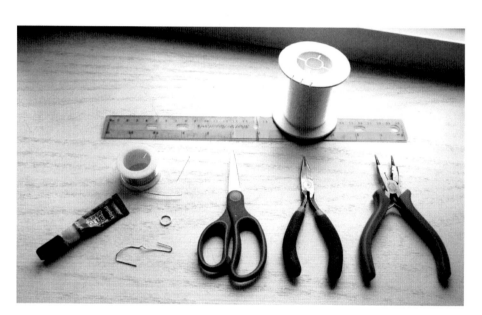

What you will need:

filament thread (fishing wire 6 gauge)
ruler (clear is helpful)
super glue (liquid, not gel)
metal wire (18 gauge)
1/2" round hoop
small scissors
pliers
round pliers with cutters
paper clip (opened up)
stars

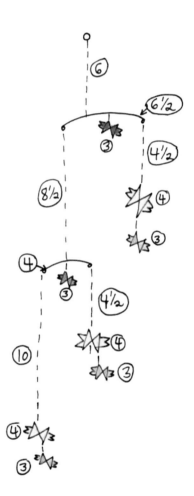

To make a mobile start by folding the stars needed. For this Antila mobile design you will need three 4" stars and five 3" stars. You can wax and glitter if desired.

Next you will need two wires for hanging. The top wire will be cut to 6.5" and the bottom will be cut to 4". You will need to loop the ends of the wires.

Next create the skeleton of the mobile. First start by tying a filament thread to the small hoop. Hang the hoop from a hook tied down far enough from the ceiling for you to work comfortably. (I use an opened paper clip hooked over my chandelier.) Then tie the thread measured 6" down to the center of the longer metal wire.

Next tie another thread to one of the loops on the end of the 6.5" metal wire. Measure that down 8.5" and tie to the center of the 4" metal wire. Leave about 1" and tie on your first 3" star. (Shown in green.) Stars are tied on using the stringing method in Chapter 3, but tied using a knot. Pull each knot tight with the pliers.

Lay out your stars in the order that you would like the to be hung. Tie three of the 3" stars to the three 4" stars, leaving about 1" in between. (Shown in yellow and blue.) Tie the opposite corner of the star with a longer filament thread that will be used to hang from mobile. Tie the last remaining 3" star with a filament thread. (Shown in pink.)

Now attach the 4"-3" star bundles at the three empty loops. The top bundle will hang down 4" from the loop. The bottom two bundles will hang down 4" and 10" from the loops.

Tie the remaining star (pink) to the top wire closer to the star bundle than the second tier.

Now to level the mobile. Start with the bottom tire and move up. Level the metal wire by sliding the knot where the green star is attached at the wire in either direction. Then move up to the top tier and level where it attaches to the hoop at the very top of the mobile.

Once all the leveling is done all the knots can be dabbed with super glue. Then once the glue is dry, the filament thread can be cut as close to the knot as possible.

Mobile complete!

Chapter 5
Flat star

Step 1

Follow the steps on how to fold a Froebel star on page one from step 1 to step 28.

Step 5

Pull tight and push flat to crease.

Step 2

Take one of the strips and loop it around on top of its same color. flipping the strip, tuck the end through the slot under the upper folded strip.

Step 6

Rotate counterclockwise a quarter of a turn and take the next strip and loop it around on top of its same color. flipping the strip, tuck the end through the slot under the upper folded strip.

Step 3

Pull tight and push flat to crease.

Step 7

Pull tight and push flat to crease.

Step 4

Rotate counterclockwise a quarter of a turn and take the next strip and loop it around on top of its same color. flipping the strip, tuck the end through the slot under the upper folded strip.

Step 8

Rotate counterclockwise a quarter of a turn and take the next strip and loop it around on top of its same color. flipping the strip, tuck the end through the slot under the upper folded strip.

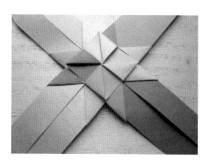

Step 9
Pull tight and push flat to crease.

Step 10
Trim edges for complete flat star.

Chapter 6
Spheres

Step 1
Follow directions on how to make a Froebel star from step 1 to step 34.

Step 4
Of the two points next to each other, crease the left strips back.

Step 2
Flip star over and cut strips off close to where they come out from the square weave.

You will need six stars completed like this.

Step 3
Flip star back over and trim ends of strips.

Step 5
To interlock the stars, looking at the backsides, line two stars up together and take the points that are folded back and tuck them in the slot behind the point that stand straight up.

Star with one flat side.

Front sides of two joined together.

Step 6
Join a third star by interlocking the points in the same way. Start in the corner,

and work your way outward.

Make sure to get the points tucked far enough inside so that you can't see them.

Step 8
The fifth star will join the cluster on three sides. Start with the center side and work your way out towards the outer sides at the same time.

Step 7
Joining the fourth star will be the same as the third.

Step 10
As you get to interlocking the last points, you will have to switch working from the inside of the star to the outside.

Step 9
The last star will join on all sides and complete the sphere. Interlock this star as you did the previous one.

Completed sphere.

I also have a youtube video at www.youtube.com/watch?v=tGBcevVfftc which is great for showing how the sphere is interlocked. There is a pinching technique that I use that is effective in tightening the sphere.

Chapter 7
Garlands

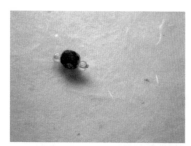

Start the garland by creating a loop in your thread. I like to use filament wire because it is unbreakable. Place a crimp bead on the thread making the loop the desired size. String beads onto garland.

Thread a needle with filament thread and pierce the star thru the middle and out the opposite side in the same spot. You may have to take a few tries at getting the needle straight thru.

String beads.

Repeat stringing stars and beads until desired length is reached.

Chapter 8
Tree toppers

Step 1
Begin star topper by choosing thickness of wire. I use 12 or 14 gauge wire.

Step 5
Taking a large star made up through step 34, fold the wire back on itself and cut slightly shorter than the thickness of the strips of paper.

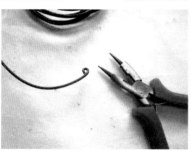

Step 2
Create a loop in the end of the wire.

Step 6
Laying the wire straight across the star, hook the end of the wire underneath the 3 dimensional star point on the adjacent side.

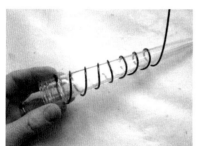

Step 3
Taking a tapered object (I use the cylinder part of a bulb baster) wrap the wire starting at the wide end up the taper to about 6 inches.

Step 7
Pinch the bend in the wire tight so that the wire does not move.

Step 4
Remove the coil and bend the wire in two places so that it goes straight into the center of the coil, then straight out away from it.

Step 8
Begin folding the remaining 3 dimensional points of the star. The upper right point will slide under the wire.

Step 9
The lower right strip will loop
around over the wire covering it up.

Step 11
The last strip will loop around
over the wire covering it up.

Step 10
The third strip will
slide under the wire.

Step 12
Trim strips.

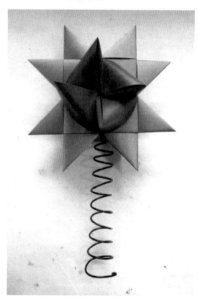

Star tree topper complete.

Sphere toppers are made in the same manner.

Step 1
Insert the straight part of a pre made topper coil through a hole in the corner of two stars and slide all the way through the center of the sphere and up and out through the perpendicular side of the sphere. Trim wire slightly shorter than the thickness of the paper strips used.

Step 2
Bend the wire at a 90 degree angle.

Sphere topper complete.

Step 3
Holding the wire from the bottom turn it so that the bent end slides inside the sphere by disappearing inside a tucked in point.

Step 4
Give the bent wire a pinch to tighten in place.

Chapter 9
Crosses & Wreathes

Making crosses and wreathes are both made in the same way. First start by taking the number of stars you will need to complete the piece.

Cross stars are connected in a straight line, while the wreath stars are connected together in a curving line.

Open the inside of a star's tips by giving a gentile squeeze and wiggling the corner points of another star inside the spaces. (place a small dab of glue in the middle of the corner points that are going inside the other star.)

Slide the stars together until the inside corner points disappear inside the other star.

Work your way all the way around the wreath connecting stars until you join the first star with the last star.

Repeat this method for all the stars until you have your finished piece.

You may wax, glitter, and string if desired.

Chapter 10
Hearts

Step 1
Follow steps 1 thru 13 on how to fold a star.

Step 5
Pull tight and crease.

Step 2
Take bottom left strip and tuck it through the loop on the right corner of the square weave.

Step 6
Flip over.

Step 3
Pull tight and crease.

Step 7
Take bottom left strip and tuck it through the loop on the right corner of the square weave.

Step 4
Take the upper right strip and tuck it through the top loop on the square weave.

Step 8
Pull tight and crease.

Step 9
Take the upper right strip and tuck it through the top loop on the square weave.

Step 13
Taking the bottom right strip and flipping forward, tuck the end into the adjacent top of the outside square weave. Insert as far as the width of the strip.

Step 10
Pull tight and crease.

Step 11
Trim strips parallel to the square weave about 6 inches long.

Step 14
Flip over.

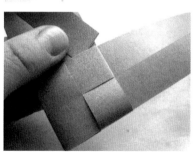

Step 12
Taking the bottom left strip and flipping forward, tuck the end into the adjacent top of the outside square weave. Insert as far as the width of the strip.

Step 15
Taking the upper left strip and flipping it backward, tuck the end into the adjacent top of the outside square weave. Insert as far as the width of the strip.

Step 16
Taking the upper right strip and flipping it backward, tuck the end into the adjacent top of the outside square weave. Insert as far as the width of the strip.

Step 17
You can place a dab of glue on the ends of the strips that tuck inside the heart if you desire. Heart complete.

Chapter 11
Speciality & Recycled Papers

Cutting and using custom paper is done by creating long enough strips by taping shorter pieces together. In order for the strips to be long enough they should be 25 times longer than the width. So if you are using 3/4" thick strips they should be almost 19" long. Vintage paper can be used, just make sure it isn't too brittle that it tears when you fold it.

When using thin paper, like newspaper, it is best to double up and use two strips instead of one.

Using one sided paper requires some cutting, flipping the paper, and taping back in place.

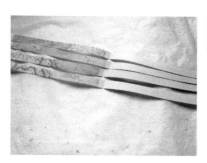

Start your paper by taping two strips together. One strip will be the printed side and the other strip will be the plain reverse side.

Tape strip back together after flipping it over to leave the printed side facing up.

Fold the strips in the middle, offsetting the taped section.

Complete all points the same way.

View of the back side of the strips.

Finish the star as you normally would.

Fold points and before sliding the strip through the loop, cut.

Spheres are made using this method also.

About the Author:
Frances Martin lives in north-east Ohio with her husband and two boys.
She owns and operates her own business at theStarcraft.etsy.com where
you can buy paper supplies for making your own stars. She also enjoys
yoga, running, and nutrition.

Made in the USA
Las Vegas, NV
12 November 2021